Special Tuning

1800c.c. Engine

MGB

THE M.G. CAR COMPANY LIMITED

Proprietors: Morris Motors Limited

ABINGDON-ON-THAMES

Telephone: Abingdon 251-2-3-4   *Telegrams:* Emgee, Abingdon

Sole Exporters

NUFFIELD EXPORTS LIMITED

Proprietors: Morris Motors Limited

COWLEY - OXFORD - ENGLAND

Phone: Oxford, England, 77733   *Telex:* 83133 Morex, Oxford, England
Cables: Morex, Oxford, England

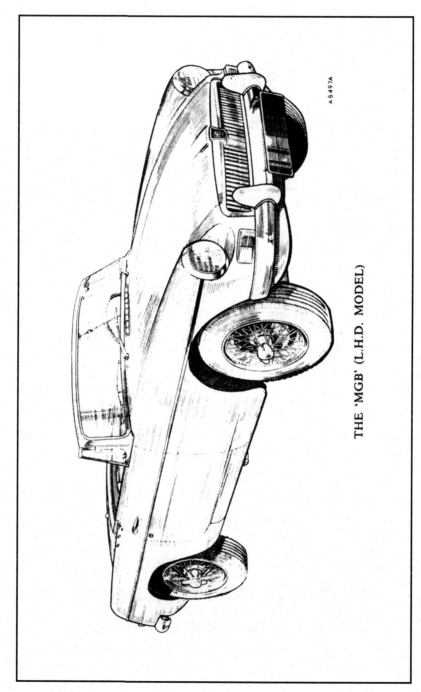

A 8497 A

THE 'MGB' (L.H.D. MODEL)

CONTENTS

FOREWORD

This is another of the M.G. Tuning Booklets which have been issued in recent years. It deals specifically with the Series MGB.

The 'MGB' as delivered from the Factory in its standard form is tuned to give maximum performance with 100-octane gasoline consistent with complete reliability and reasonable freedom from pinking. There is, however, a more or less continuous demand from enthusiasts all over the world for information on methods of improving the performance for competitive purposes, and it is to meet this demand that this booklet has been prepared.

It must be clearly understood, however, that, whereas it is a simple matter to increase the power output of the engine, this increase in power must inevitably carry with it a tendency to reduce reliability. It is for this reason that the terms of the Warranty on a new M.G. expressly exclude any super-tuning of the kind described in this booklet, but this does not mean that tuning in this way will necessarily make the car hopelessly unreliable. In fact, it may be assumed that it will be at least as reliable as other cars of similar performance.

This booklet is laid out to give details for progressively increasing the power. With the above ideas firmly in mind, the owner should select the simplest tuning method which will give him the performance he requires, remembering all the time that here, as elsewhere, **Power Costs Money**.

Tuning hints are included for the racing enthusiasts who want to go to the limit and who have facilities to modify or make up special parts for their cars. We hope this section will be of use to them.

Owners are reminded that in certain countries noise restriction regulations are in force. The Company cannot therefore accept responsibility for any increase in the existing noise level of the car which may result after special tuning operations have been carried out.

GETTING THE BEST FROM YOUR 'MGB'

When fitted with a H.C. engine (compression ratio 8·8 : 1)

The engine fitted to your 'MGB' is a highly developed unit and it is essential that you should know something about the specialized maintenance it requires if you are to maintain it at the peak of its mechanical efficiency.

Special recommendations on the sparking plugs, ignition settings, and fuel to be used are given by the manufacturers, and it is stressed that failures are bound to occur if these are not strictly adhered to. Particular care is needed with this engine owing to its high compression ratio, which makes it extremely sensitive to variations in fuel, ignition timing, and the heat range of the sparking plugs.

In lower compression engines a much wider range of fuels can be tolerated without causing serious damage to the engine, and ignition settings will stand variations of a reasonable amount. Also, even if the incorrect sparking plugs are used, no more damage may be incurred than burnt-out plugs or leaky valves. But with an engine having a very high compression ratio the range of fuels, sparking plugs, and ignition settings is much narrower and it is essential that the mixture should always be correct, and particularly never overweak at maximum load or power.

High-compression engines are very sensitive to variations in spark advance (over-advance) and to fuel/air ratio (mixture). Variations in these settings will increase the combustion temperature, and if the variation is excessive pre-ignition will cause high shock waves, resulting in damage to the engine. The engine should be decarbonized at regular intervals as excessive deposits of ash from the combustion of lubricating oil and fuel can cause pre-ignition difficulties.

Choice of fuel
When fitted with H.C. engine (compression ratio 8·8 : 1)

The octane number of a motor fuel is an indication given by the fuel technicians of its knock resistance. High-octane fuels have been produced to improve the efficiency of engines by allowing them to operate on high compression ratios, resulting in better fuel economy and greater power. Owing to the high compression ratio of the 'MGB' engines, fuels with an octane rating below 98 are not suitable; should it be necessary to use a fuel with a lower octane number, the car must be used very carefully until the correct fuel can be obtained.

It is necessary to use Super grade fuels in the 100-octane range unless Premium fuels of minimum 98-octane Research are available.

When fitted with L.C. engine (compression ratio 8·0 : 1)

Premium fuels of minimum 93-octane Research up to 97 octane are required, with preference to 95/97.

Super grade fuels in the 100-octane range can be used if preferred.

Sparking plugs

The correct grade of sparking plug for use under normal driving conditions is the Champion N–9Y. Plugs of a lower heat range (hotter running) should not be used, otherwise pre-ignition will occur, with consequent rise in combustion temperature and resulting engine damage. For competition work or hard driving where high output is consistently sustained the Champion N3 sparking plug should be used. This is a cooler-running plug and will ensure lower combustion temperatures and an increased margin of safety. Accumulated deposits of carbon, leaking or cracked insulators, and thin electrodes are all causes of pre-ignition. The plugs should therefore be examined, cleaned, and adjusted at the specified intervals and defective ones renewed. New plugs should be fitted every 12,000 miles (20000 km.).

Static ignition settings

It is of the utmost importance that the correct setting should always be maintained. It will be appreciated that any variation in the contact breaker gap will affect the ignition setting, and your particular attention is called to the 6,000 miles (10000 km.) check and adjustment of the distributor points specified in the Driver's Handbook. After adjusting the contact breaker gap to the correct setting it is advisable to check the ignition timing, and to correct it if necessary.

An accurate check can be carried out by a very simple electrical method. To do this, connect a 12-volt lamp between the low-tension terminal on the side of the distributor and a good earth point on the engine.

With the ignition switched on and the sparking plugs removed, turn the crankshaft until the crankshaft pulley pointer is exactly at the correct number of degrees as stated under 'GENERAL DATA'.

If the ignition timing is correct the lamp will light at exactly this point. Any discrepancy in the ignition setting can be rectified by turning the vernier adjusting nut on the distributor until the test lamp lights at exactly the correct setting. If pinking should occur due to the use of a fuel of a lower range than our recommendations, retarding the ignition 2 to 3° can be tolerated. In no circumstances should the ignition be advanced beyond the correct setting.

Dunlop centre-lock wheel

This is built on the Rudge-Whitworth system and provides the most rapid method of changing road wheels. Like all mechanical devices, it must be properly treated in order to give 100 per cent service.

Observation of the following quite simple hints will ensure complete satisfaction.

When the car is new. After the first long run, or after 50 miles (80 km.) of short runs, jack up each wheel and hammer the nuts to ensure that they are tight.

When wheels are replaced, cover both conical surfaces and the serrations in the hub, also the coned surface and threads in the locknut, with a light coating of grease. Hammer tight and repeat as when car is new.

When a forced change is made on the road, remove and grease the hub as soon as convenient.

Once in 12 months remove the wheels for examination and regreasing.

When changing wheels wipe the serrations and cones on the hub, wheel, and locknut to remove any foreign matter that would prevent the wheel from properly seating. Rust and dirt are the enemies of all mechanical devices.

GETTING THE BEST FROM YOUR 'MGB'

After a general overhaul of the car, which may involve stripping of the axle, the inscription on the locknuts should be checked to see that it corresponds with the side of the car on which it is applied.

General.—Always hammer the locknuts tight. Lift the car on the jack before using the hammer. The locknuts are designed for self-locking, but they should not on that account be permitted to run untightened, because there is, in such case, a possibility of damaging the splines.

GENERAL DATA

Engine

Type	18G
Number of cylinders ..	4
Bore	3·16 in. (80·26 mm.)
Stroke	3·5 in. (89 mm.)
Capacity	1798 c.c. (109·8 cu. in.)
Firing order	1, 3, 4, 2
Compression ratio	H.C. 8·8 : 1 (L.C. 8 : 1)
Capacity of combustion chamber (valves fitted) ..	42·5 to 43·5 c.c. (2·59 to 2·65 cu. in.)
Valve operation ..	Overhead by push-rod
Safe maximum r.p.m. ..	6,000
Valve crash r.p.m.	6,230
B.H.P.	H.C. 95 (L.C. 91) at 5,400
B.M.E.P.	152 at 3,100
Torque (lb. ft.)	
H.C.	110 (15·2 kg. m.) at 3,000 r.p.m.
L.C.	105 (14·5 kg. m.) at 3,000 r.p.m.
Octane rating	Minimum requirements for knock-free operation. H.C. 98+, L.C. 93+
Cooling system	Thermo-siphon, pump- and fan-assisted
Oversize bore	
First	·010 in. (·254 mm.)
Maximum	·040 in. (1·016 mm.)

Crankshaft

Main journal diameter ..	2·126 to 2·127 in. (54·01 to 54·02 mm.)
Minimum regrind diameter..	2·086 in. (52·984 mm.)
Crankpin journal diameter..	1·8759 to 1·8764 in. (47·65 to 47·66 mm.)
Crankpin minimum regrind diameter	1·8359 in. (46·64 mm.)

Main bearings

Number and type	3 shell type
Material	
Bottom half	Steel-backed copper-lead
Top half	Steel-backed copper-lead
Length	1·125 in. (28·575 mm.)
End-clearance	·002 to ·003 in. (·051 to ·076 mm.)
End-thrust	Taken by thrust washers at centre main bearing
Running clearance	·001 to ·0027 in. (·025 to ·0688 mm.)

Connecting rods

Length between centres	..	6·5 in. (165·1 mm.)
Big-end bearings		
Material top half	..	Steel-backed copper-lead
Material bottom half	..	Steel-backed copper-lead
Bearing side-clearance	..	·008 to ·012 in. (·203 to ·305 mm.)
Bearing diametrical clearance	.. .. ..	·001 to ·0027 in. (·025 to ·0688 mm.)

Pistons

Type ..	.. .. ..	Aluminium alloy
Clearances		
Bottom of skirt	.. ..	·0018 to ·0024 in. (·045 to ·060 mm.)
Top of skirt	.. ..	·0036 to ·0048 in. (·091 to ·121 mm.)
Oversizes	.. .. ..	+·010 in., +·020 in. +·030 in., +·040 in. (+·254 mm., +·508 mm., +·762 mm., +1·016 mm.)

Piston rings

Compression: Plain	..	Top ring (chrome-plated)
Tapered	..	Second and third rings
Width	.. .. ..	·0615 to ·0625 in. (1·56 to 1·58 mm.)
Thickness ..	.. ..	·137 in. (3·48 mm.)
Fitted gap	.. ..	·012 to ·017 in. (·304 to ·431 mm.)
Clearance in groove	..	·0015 to ·0035 in. (·038 to ·089 mm.)
Oil control ring	.. ..	Slotted scraper
Width	.. .. ..	·1552 to ·1562 in. (3·94 to 3·99 mm.)
Thickness ..	.. ..	·137 in. (3·48 mm.)
Fitted gap	.. ..	·012 to ·017 in. (·304 to ·431 mm.)
Clearance in groove	..	·0016 to ·0036 in. (·040 to ·091 mm.)

Gudgeon pin

Type ..	.. .. ..	Clamped
Fit ..	.. .. ..	Free fit to 20° C. (68° F.)
Diameter	.. ..	·75 in. (19·05 mm.)

Cylinder head

Cylinder head depth	..	$3\frac{11}{16}\,{}^{+·015}_{-·000}$ in. ($80·6\,{}^{+·400}_{-·000}$ mm.)
Thickness of cylinder head gasket	.. .. ..	·023 in. (·584 mm.) compressed
Capacity of cylinder head gasket	.. .. ..	3·208 c.c.

9

GENERAL DATA

Cylinder head—*continued*

Capacity of combustion space	42·5/43·5 c.c. (valves fitted)
Capacity of piston head below block face	H.C. 10·87 c.c. (L.C. 17·43 c.c.)
Capacity of piston concavity	H.C. 6·25 c.c. (L.C. 12·8 c.c.)
Capacity of plug centre hole	·2 c.c.
Inlet and exhaust manifold gasket	Part No. 1G 2417
Valve seat angle in cylinder head	45°

Valves and valve gear

Seat angle	
Inlet and exhaust ..	45½° (seat angle in cylinder head 45°)
Head diameter	
Inlet	1·562 to 1·567 in. (38·67 to 38·8 mm.)
Exhaust	1·343 to 1·348 in. (34·11 to 34·23 mm.)
Stem diameter	
Inlet	·3422 to ·3427 in. (8·692 to 8·709 mm.)
Exhaust	·34175 to ·34225 in. (8·680 to 8·693 mm.)
Valve lift (clearance set ·015 in.)	·3645 in. (9·26 mm.)
Cam lift	·250 in. (6·35 mm.)
Throat diameter	
Inlet	1·3125 in. (33·33 mm.)
Exhaust	1·156 in. (29·36 mm.)
Valve stem to guide clearance	
Inlet	·00155 to ·00255 in. (·0394 to ·0648 mm.)
Exhaust	·00200 to ·00300 in. (·051 to ·076 mm.)
Valve rocker clearance	
Running	·015 in. (·38 mm.) cold
Timing	
Inlet and exhaust ..	·021 in. (·53 mm.)
Timing markings	Dimples on timing wheels
Chain pitch and number of pitches	⅜ in. (9·52 mm.), 52 pitches
Inlet valve	
Opens	16° B.T.D.C.
Closes	56° A.B.D.C.
Exhaust valve	
Opens	51° B.B.D.C.
Closes	21° A.T.D.C.

Valve guides

Length

  Inlet   ..   ..   .. $1\frac{5}{8}$ in. (41·275 mm.)

  Exhaust   ..   ..   .. $2\frac{14}{64}$ in. (56·96 mm.)

Diameter

Inlet and exhaust

  Outside ..   ..   ..   ·5635 to ·5640 in. (14·3129 to 14·3256 mm.)

  Inside   ..   ..   ..   ·34425 to ·34475 in. (8·74269 to 8·75665 mm.)

Fitted height above head   ..   ·625 in. (15·87 mm.)

Valve springs

Free length

  Inner   ..   ..   .. $1\frac{31}{32}$ in. (50 mm.)

  Outer   ..   ..   .. $2\frac{9}{64}$ in. (54·372 mm.)

Fitted length

  Inner   ..   ..   .. $1\frac{7}{16}$ in. (36·51 mm.)

  Outer   ..   ..   .. $1\frac{9}{16}$ in. (39·69 mm.)

Number of working coils

  Inner   ..   ..   .. $6\frac{1}{2}$

  Outer   ..   ..   .. $4\frac{1}{2}$

Pressure

  Valve open   ..   ..   Inner 50 lb. (22·7 kg.)

    Outer 117 lb. (53·08 kg.)

  Valve closed   ..   ..   Inner 30 lb. (13·6 kg.)

    Outer $72\frac{1}{2}$ lb. (32·89 kg.)

Tappets

Type ..   ..   Flat base. Barrel type

Diameter

  Body   ..   ..   .. $\frac{13}{16}$ in. (20·64 mm.)

  Working face   ..   .. $\frac{9}{16}$ in. (14·29 mm.)

Length   ..   ..   ..   2·293 to 2·303 in. (58·25 to 58·5 mm.)

Rockers

Outside diameter before fit-
ting)   ..   ..   ..   ·751 in. (19·07 mm.)

Inside diameter (reamed in
position) ..   ..   ..   ·616 to ·620 in. (15·65 to 15·74 mm.)

Bore of rocker arms   ..   ·7485 to ·7495 in. (19·01 to 19·04 mm.)

Rocker ratio   ..   ..   1·426 : 1

GENERAL DATA

Camshaft
Journal diameters

Front	..	..	.. 1·78875 to 1·78925 in. (45·43 to 45·44 mm.)
Centre	..	..	.. 1·72875 to 1·72925 in. (43·91 to 43·92 mm.)
Rear	. ..	..	.. 1·62275 to 1·62325 in. (41·22 to 41·23 mm.)

End-float .. .. .. ·003 to ·007 in. (·076 to ·178 mm.)

Bearings—number and type 3. Thinwall steel-backed copper-lead

Outside diameter (before fitting)

Front	..	..	.. 1·920 in. (48·76 mm.)
Centre	..	..	.. 1·860 in. (47·24 mm.)
Rear	..	..	.. 1·754 in. (44·55 mm.)

Inside diameter (reamed in position)

Front	..	..	.. 1·79025 to 1·79075 in. (45·472 to 45·485 mm.)
Centre	..	..	.. 1·73025 to 1·73075 in. (43·948 to 43·961 mm.)
Rear	..	..	.. 1·62425 to 1·62475 in. (41·256 to 41·269 mm.)

Diametrical clearance .. ·001 to ·002 in. (·0254 to ·0508 mm.)

Engine lubrication system
Oil pump

Type .. .. .. Eccentric rotor

Relief pressure valve

operates .. .. 70 lb./sq. in. (4·9 kg./cm.^{2})

Relief valve spring

Free length .. .. 3 in. (76·2 mm.)

Fitted length .. .. 2$\frac{4}{16}$ in. (54·77 mm.) at 16 lb. (7·26 kg.) load

Identification colour .. Red spot

Oil filter

Type .. .. .. Tecalemit

Capacity .. .. .. $\frac{1}{2}$ pint (·6 U.S. pint, ·28 litre)

Oil pressure

Normal running

Minimum .. .. 10 lb./sq. in. (·7 kg./cm.^{2})

Maximum .. .. 80 lb./sq. in. (5·6 kg./cm.^{2})

Torque wrench settings

Cylinder head nuts	45–50 lb. ft. (6·16–6·91 kg. m.)
Main bearing nuts	70 lb. ft. (9·7 kg. m.)
Connecting rod set screws ..	40–45 lb. ft. (5·5–6·2 kg. m.)
Clutch assembly to flywheel	25–30 lb. ft. (3·4–4·1 kg. m.)
Flywheel bolts	40 lb. ft. (5·5 kg. m.)
Gudgeon pin set screws ..	25 lb. ft. (3·4 kg. m.)

Fuel system

Carburetter

Make and type	S.U. twin HS4 semi-downdraught
Diameter	1½ in. (38·1 mm.)
Needle	MB (standard), No. 6 (rich), No. 21 (weak)
Jet	·090 in. (2·29 mm.)
Carburetter piston ..	Part No. AUC 2061
Piston spring ..	Red (Part No. AUC 4387)

Air cleaner

Make and type	Coopers Mechanical Joints Ltd., Steel canister, paper element (replaceable)

Fuel pump

Make and type	S.U. electric, high-pressure
Delivery test	10 gal. per hr. (12 U.S. gal., 45·4 litres per hr.)
Suction lift	33 in. (83·8 cm.)
Output lift	48 in. (121·9 cm.)

Cooling system

Type	Pressurized radiator, thermo-siphon, pump- and fan-assisted
Filler cap spring pressure ..	7 lb. (3·175 kg.)
Thermostat setting	70·5 to 75·6° C. (159 to 168° F.)
Quantity of anti-freeze	
15° frost	1 pint (1·2 U.S. pints, ·57 litre)
25° frost	1½ pints (1·8 U.S. pints, ·85 litre)
35° frost	2 pints (2·4 U.S. pints, 1·1 litres)

Ignition system

Sparking plugs	Champion N–9Y
Size	14 mm.
Plug gap	·024 to ·026 in. (·61 to ·66 mm.)
Coil	Lucas HA12
Distributor	Lucas, Type 25D4
Distributor contact points gap	·014 to ·016 in. (·35 to ·40 mm.)
Suppressors type	Lucas No. 78106A fitted on each H.T. cable
Timing	H.C. 10° B.T.D.C. (L.C. 8° B.T.D.C.)

Clutch

Make and type	Borg & Beck 8 in. (20·3 cm.) diaphragm spring. Strap drive

GENERAL DATA

Clutch—*continued*

Diameter	.. .. ..	8 in. (20·3 cm.)
Facing material	.. ..	Wound yarn—Borglite
Damper springs	.. ..	6
Colour	.. .. ..	Maroon/light green

Gearbox (Standard and Overdrive)

Number of forward speeds	..	4
Synchromesh	.. ..	Second, third, and fourth gears
Overdrive	.. .. ..	·802

Ratios

Top	.. .. ..	1·0000 : 1
Third	.. .. ..	1·3736 : 1
Second	.. .. ..	2·2143 : 1
First	.. .. ..	3·6363 : 1
Reverse	.. .. ..	4·7552 : 1

Overall ratios			*M.p.h. per 1,000 r.p.m.*
Overdrive	.. .. ..	3·135 : 1	22·3
Top	.. .. ..	3·909 : 1	17·9
Third	.. .. ..	5·36 : 1	13·09
Second	.. .. ..	8·65 : 1	8·11
First	.. .. ..	14·20 : 1	4·94
Reverse	.. .. ..	18·60 : 1	3·77

Speedometer gears ratio .. 9 : 28 (overdrive 5 : 16)

Optional axle ratios			*Overall ratios*	*M.p.h. per 1,000 r.p.m.*
Overdrive	.. .. ..		3·649 : 1	19·2
Top	.. .. ..		4·55 : 1	15·4
Third	.. .. ..		6·24 : 1	11·24
Second	.. .. ..		9·98 : 1	7·03
First	.. .. ..		16·54 : 1	4·24
Reverse	.. .. ..		21·63 : 1	·3·24
Overdrive	.. .. ..		3·449 : 1	20·3
Top	.. .. ..		4·3 : 1	16·3
Third	.. .. ..		5·9 : 1	11·89
Second	.. .. ..		9·52 : 1	7·37
First	.. .. ..		15·63 : 1	4·4
Reverse	.. .. ..		20·44 : 1	3·43
Overdrive	.. .. ..		3·288 : 1	21·3
Top	.. .. ..		4·1 : 1	17·1
Third	.. .. ..		5·63 : 1	12·44
Second	.. .. ..		9·07 : 1	7·73
First	.. .. ..		14·90 : 1	4·70
Reverse	.. .. ..		19·49 : 1	3·60

Gearbox (close-ratio)   *Non-overdrive and Overdrive*

Number of forward speeds ..   4

Synchromesh   ..   ..   Second, third, and fourth gears

Overdrive ratio   ..   ..   ·802

Ratios

Top	1·0	: 1
Third	1·268	: 1
Second	1·620	: 1
First	2·450	: 1
Reverse	4·7552	: 1

Overall ratios   *M.p.h. per 1,000 r.p.m.*

Overdrive	3·135 : 1	22·3
Top	3·909 : 1	17·9
Third	4·956 : 1	14·1
Second	6·332 : 1	11·0
First	9·577 : 1	7·3
Reverse	18·588 : 1	3·7

Speedometer gears ratio   ..   9 : 28 (Overdrive 5 : 16)

Optional axle ratios   *Overall ratios*   *M.p.h. per 1,000 r.p.m.*

Overdrive	3·649 : 1	19·2
Top	4·55 : 1	15·4
Third	5·769 : 1	12·1
Second	7·371 : 1	9·5
First	11·147 : 1	6·3
Reverse	21·635 : 1	3·2
Overdrive	3·449 : 1	20·3
Top	4·30 : 1	16·3
Third	5·452 : 1	12·8
Second	6·966 : 1	10·0
First	10·535 : 1	6·6
Reverse	20·447 : 1	3·4
Overdrive	3·288 : 1	21·3
Top	4·10 : 1	17·1
Third	5·198 : 1	13·4
Second	6·642 : 1	10·5
First	10·045 : 1	7·0
Reverse	19·496 : 1	3·6

Steering

Type ..   ..   Rack and pinion

Steering-wheel

     Turns—lock to lock   ..   2·93

     Diameter ..   ..   ..   16¼ in. (41·9 cm.)

Camber angle   ..   ..   Front 1°

GENERAL DATA

Steering—*continued*

Castor angle	7°
King-pin inclination ..	8°
Toe-in	$\frac{1}{16}$ to $\frac{3}{32}$ in. (1·6 to 2·4 mm.)
Track	
Front	Disc wheels 49 in. (1·244 m.) Wire wheels 49¼ in. (1·251 m.)
Rear	Disc wheels 49¼ in. (1·251 m.) Wire wheels 49¼ in. (1·251 m.)

Front suspension

Type	Independent coil
Spring detail	
Coil diameter (mean) ..	3·238 in. (82·23 mm.)
Diameter of wire	·498 in. (12·66 mm.)
Free height	9·9 $\pm$ $\frac{1}{16}$ in. (25·14 cm. $\pm$1·6 mm.)
Number of free coils ..	7·5
Static laden length ..	7 $\pm$ $\frac{1}{32}$ in. (177·8 cm. $\pm$·8 mm.)
Static laden length at load of	1,030 lb. (467·2 kg.)
Maximum deflection ..	4·34 in. (11·02 cm.)
Dampers (front)	Piston type

Rear suspension

	Early type	Later type
Type	Semi-elliptic	
Spring detail		
Number of leaves ..	5 and bottom plate	2 top and bottom plate at $\frac{3}{32}$ in. (5·6 mm.), three at $\frac{3}{16}$ in. (4·8 mm.)
Width of leaves	1¾ in. (44·45 mm.)	1¾ in. (44·45 mm.)
Gauge	$\frac{7}{32}$ in. (5·56 mm.)	$\frac{7}{32}$ in. (5·56 mm.) and $\frac{3}{16}$ in. (4·8 mm.)
Working load	400 lb. (181·44 kg.)	450 lb. (204·12 kg.)
Free camber	4·04 in. (102·6 mm.)	4·83 to 5·11 in. (122·68 to 129·79 mm.)
Dampers (rear)	Piston type	

Propeller shaft

Type	Tubular flanged 1100 series
Make and type of joints ..	Hardy Spicer, needle roller
Propeller shaft length (between centres of joints) ..	27⅝ in. (70·167 cm.) standard 28¾ in. (73·025 cm.) overdrive

Propeller shaft—*continued*

Overall length	.. .. ..	30 in. (76·2 cm.) standard
		31⅛ in. (79·057 cm.) overdrive
Diameter	.. .. ..	2 in. (50·8 mm.)

Rear axle

Make and type	.. ..	B.M.C. 'B' type, three-quarter-floating
Ratio		
Standard ..	.. ..	11/43
Optional ..	.. ..	9/41, 10/43, 10/41
Adjustment ..	.. ..	Shims

Electrical equipment

System	.. .. ..	12-volt. Positive earth
Charging system	.. ..	Compensated voltage control
Battery	.. .. ..	Two 6-volt Lucas SG9E
Starter motor	.. ..	Lucas 4-brush M418G
Dynamo	.. .. ..	Lucas C40/1

Brakes

Type ..	.. .. ..	Lockheed hydraulic (front and rear)
Front	.. .. ..	Disc 10¾ in. dia. (27·3 cm.)
Rear ..	.. .. ..	Drum 10 in. (25·4 cm.), single leading shoe
Rear linings ..	..	10 in. × 1¾ in. (25·4 cm. × 44·45 mm.)
Lining dimensions ..		9·6 in. × 1¾ in. (24·38 cm. × 44·45 mm.)
Lining area		
Front pads	.. ..	20 sq. in. (129·03 cm.²) total
Rear	.. ..	67·2 sq. in. (433·55 cm.²)
Material		
Front	.. ..	DON 55
Rear	.. ..	DON 24
Brake cylinder diameter		
Front	.. ..	2⅛ in. (53·97 mm.) dia.
Rear	.. ..	·80 in. (20·32 mm.) dia.

Wheels

Type		
Ventilated disc	.. ..	4J × 14 in.
Wire (optional)	..	4½J × 14- and 60-spoke

Tyres .. | .. .. | Minimum tyre pressures, set cold

Standard		
Size	.. ..	5·60 × 14 (Tubed) Dunlop Gold Seal Nylon C.41 front and rear

GENERAL DATA

Tyres—*continued*

Pressures	Normal motoring, including sustained speeds on motorways up to 90 m.p.h. (145 km.p.h.) 18 lb./sq. in. (1·27 kg./cm.²) For maximum or near-maximum speed and sustained speeds in excess of 90 m.p.h. (145 km.p.h.) 24 lb./sq. in. (1·69 kg./cm.²) (front and rear)
Optional	
Size	5·90 × 14 Dunlop Road Speed R.S.5
Pressures	All conditions (except Competition work) 18 lb./sq. in. (1·27 kg./cm.²) (front and rear)

Note.—Rear tyre pressures may be increased by 2 lb./sq. in. (·14 kg./cm.²) with advantage when touring with a laden boot.

For competition work, advice on tyre pressures, etc., may be obtained direct from the Dunlop Rubber Co. Ltd., Fort Dunlop, Erdington, Birmingham 24.

Capacities	*Imp.*	*U.S.A.*	*Litres*
Engine sump (incl. filter) ..	7½ pts.	9 pts.	4·28
Gearbox	5½ pts.	6¾ pts.	3·12
Rear axle	2¾ pts.	3¼ pts.	1·56
Cooling system (with heater)	10 pts.	12 pts.	5·67
Steering rack	⅓ pt.	·39 pt.	·19
Fuel tank	10 gal.	12 gal.	45·4
Brake system	1 pt.	1·2 pt.	·568
Oil cooler	¾ pt.	·9 pt.	·42

General dimensions	
Wheelbase	91 in. (231·14 cm.)
Over-all length	153 3/16 in. (389·13 cm.)
Over-all width	59 15/16 in. (152·28 cm.)
Over-all height	49⅜ in. (125·41 cm.)
Ground clearance	5 in. (12·70 cm.)
Weight: fully equipped with tools, spare wheel, oil, water, and 2 gal. (2·5 U.S. gal., 9·1 litres) of fuel ..	1,972 lb. (894·48 kg.)
Turning circles	32 ft. (9·754 m.)

TUNING

Stage 1

Tuning by port polishing (ordinary road work)

An increase of some 3 b.h.p. can be had by general attention to the cylinder head and port polishing as detailed below.

Lightly grind and polish the exhaust and inlet ports throughout. They should not be ground out so heavily that the shape or valve choke diameters are impaired, as the wall between the exhaust and inlet valves may become too thin and cause valve seat cracking.

Just inside the ports, at the bridge between the exhaust and inlet valve seats, you will notice a protuberance; do not grind too much of this away, as this is the port wall, where the water cooling has been brought down as close to the valve seats as possible.

Grind out the combustion spaces, but only very lightly, as these are already quite clean and partly machined; remove any frazes and lightly polish all over. It is most important that no enlargement around the combustion walls takes place as this may cause the cylinder head gasket to overlap. This will destroy the efficiency of the seal, lower the compression ratio, and cause tuning to be ineffective.

The combustion space and ports are already highly developed from a flow angle aspect, and it will be found difficult to improve by reshaping or enlarging. The main requirement is to obtain the highest polish, but to remove the minimum amount of metal.

Match up, by grinding, all the exhaust and inlet manifold ports with the cylinder head ports.

Grind out and polish the inlet manifold, also matching the carburetter bore. Make the bore of the manifold a gradual taper from the carburetter end to the cylinder head port, grinding away any ridges left by machining during manufacture.

Distributor setting as standard.

Stage 2

Tuning for middle-range acceleration (ordinary road work)

If most importance is placed on initial and middle-range acceleration an improvement of 2 or 3 b.h.p. may be gained in the lower ranges by fitting cam-shaft Part No. 484184. This has the timing: inlet opens 5° B.T.D.C., inlet closes 45° A.B.D.C., exhaust opens 40° B.B.D.C., exhaust closes 10° A.T.D.C.

The valve lift is ·322 in. (8·2 mm.).

Top end performance will only be slightly impaired between 5,000 and 6,000 r.p.m.

If desired, the head may be tuned by port polishing as laid down in Stage 1.

Distributor setting as standard.

TUNING

Stage 3
Compression ratio 9·6 to 9·8 : 1 (competition tune)

Carry out Stage 1.

Fit a competition (half-race) camshaft (Part No. AEH 714). This gives ·250 in. (6·35 mm.) cam lift with a 268° period for inlet and exhaust. Inlet opens 24° B.T.D.C. and closes 64° A.B.D.C. Exhaust opens 59° B.B.D.C. and closes 29° A.T.D.C.

Tappet setting ·017 in. (·43 mm.) hot. For valve springs see page 26.

Machine $\frac{1}{16}$ in. (1·59 mm.) from the cylinder head face to raise the compression ratio to 9·7 : 1. The head thickness will then be $3\frac{7}{64} \, {}^{+·015}_{-·000}$ in. $(79 \, {}^{+·38}_{-·000} \, \text{mm.})$.

Fit 1¾ in. (44·45 mm.) dia. S.U. carburetters (Part No. AUC 780); these are fitted with ·100 jets and KW needles, and light blue springs. Remove the KW needles and fit SY (Part No. AUD 1338).

A new inlet manifold (Part No. AEH 200) will be required. This manifold has a $\frac{5}{8}$ in. (15·87 mm.) dia. by-pass hole in the balance pipe. Polish this manifold as explained in Stage 1.

To prevent vibration of the carburetters it is advisable to use a synthetic rubber gasket (Part No. AHH 5791) between the carburetter and the manifold and a $\frac{1}{8}$ in. (3·18 mm.) thick double-coil spring washer (Part No. AJD 7742) under the carburetter fixing nuts so that the carburetters may be left not quite tightened solid. Wire the nuts in pairs to prevent them becoming slack. Set the fuel levels as reasonably high as possible.

No air cleaners are arranged for these carburetters, but extension pipes Part No. AHH 7209 may be used for the rear and Part No. AHH 7219 for the front.

Check the valves at full lift to ensure that the exhaust valves do not foul the top face of the cylinder block; if so, the block must be undercut to clear the valve head and give a minimum lift clearance of $\frac{1}{16}$ in. (1·59 mm.). Use a 1$\frac{13}{16}$ in. dia. flat cutter with a $\frac{1}{16}$ in. (1·59 mm.) radius at the corner of the cutter.

The engine should give 105/108 b.h.p. at 6,000 r.p.m.

The static setting for the standard distributor should be 10° B.T.D.C.

Stage 3A
Compression ratio 9·6 to 9·8 : 1 (competition tune)

As Stage 3, but alternative to machining the cylinder head, as Stage 3, the compression ratio may be raised by fitting the flat top competition pistons (as detailed in Stage 4).

Stage 3B
Compression ratio 10·5 : 1 (competition tune)

If you carry out Stage 3A the compression ratio can be raised to 10·5 : 1 by machining $\frac{1}{16}$ in. (1·59 mm.) from the cylinder head face (as detailed in Stage 3).

The engine should develop 112/115 b.h.p. at 6,000 r.p.m.

Stage 4
Compression ratio 9·3 to 9·5 : 1 (competition tune)

Polish the head as Stage 1.

Standard valves and guides may be used successfully, but for consistent performance fit bronze Hidural inlet and exhaust valve guides and the high-duty 1 ⅞ in. dia. inlet and 1 11/16 in. dia. exhaust valves in Nimonic material. The guides should be pressed into the cylinder head so that they are left standing out between 49/64 and 25/32 in. (19·45 and 19·84 mm.).

Valve seats may need re-aligning with the guides.

Use valve springs—outer (Part No. AHH 7264) and inner (Part No. AHH 7265), also the special valve cotter (pairs) (Part No. AEH 761), the valve spring top cup (Part No. AEH 760), and the bottom cup (Part No. AEH 801). Alternatively, see the use of triple valve springs on page 26.

Do not fit the metal oil shroud or the valve stem rubber oil seal that is used on the standard engine.

Standard rocker shaft and valve rockers are used, also the two centre rocker shaft brackets. The valve springs put a heavy load on the rocker shaft, especially at the ends where it is overhung, and, although it is not essential, it is desirable to fit the special front and rear rocker shaft brackets which support the end rockers from both sides (Part Nos. AEH 762 and AEH 763). Do not refit the springs which hold the rockers apart, but in place of these fit the tubular steel distance pieces leaving an end-float of ·003 to ·005 in. (·0076 to ·0127 mm.) (Part Nos. AEH 764 [1 off] and AEH 765 [2 off]).

The standard tappet adjusting screws may be used, but if the possibility of fracture is to be eliminated, then fit the special screws (Part No. AEH 766) which are solid and have no holes drilled in them; the oiling of the ball will be satisfactory without these holes.

Use the high-lift wide-period camshaft (Part No. AEH 770) with a tappet setting between valve and rocker of ·018 in. (·457 mm.) hot. This camshaft has a cam lift of ·315 in. (8·0 mm.) and a valve lift of ·452 in. (11·5 mm.). The inlet period is 300° and the exhaust 300°.

Timing is: inlet opens 50° B.T.D.C., inlet closes 70° A.B.D.C., exhaust opens 75° B.B.D.C., exhaust closes 45° A.T.D.C., with valve clearance set at ·018 in. (·46 mm.).

The high-lift, wide-period camshaft can be used with the standard push-rods and tappets satisfactorily, but cover for travel of the cam is only barely sufficient over the base of the standard tappet.

This can be overcome by boring the tappet holes in the cylinder block to a diameter of ·9375 $^{+·0005}_{-·0002}$ in. (23·81 $^{+·013}_{-·005}$ mm.) for a length of 3¼ in. (79·38 mm.) from the centre-line of the camshaft and fitting larger tappets of 15/16 in. (24 mm.) dia. (Part No. AEC 264). This will necessitate the use of shorter push-rods (Part No. AEH 767).

With the high lift of the valves it is necessary to undercut the face of the cylinder block to allow the exhaust valves full travel. This machining should be done from the valve guide centre and a flat cutter of 1 11/16 in. dia. used; the cutter should have a 1/16 in. (1·6 mm.) radius on the outer cutting corner. The undercut in the cylinder block should be 9/64 in. (3·6 mm.) deep.

For durability, when using the high-lift camshaft, it is a benefit to use the steel crankshaft and camshaft timing chain sprockets (Part Nos. AEH 769 and AEH 771).

TUNING

Stage 4—*continued*

In the centre of the cylinder head face two large core holes will be found; thread these and fit water-tight aluminium plugs, which should be faced off carefully to the head face. This will prevent water loss if the cylinder head lifts under arduous conditions.

Thread and plug the one small hole in the centre of the cylinder block face that is opposite to the cylinder head aluminium plug.

To increase water flow through the head drill out to $\frac{9}{16}$ in. (14·29 mm.) dia. the two water holes at the rear end of the cylinder block face.

Use the special cylinder head gasket.

Fit the high-compression (flat top) competition pistons (Part No. AEH 736). These pistons have large, fully floating gudgeon pins, and it is necessary to use special connecting rods (Part Nos. AEH 642 [for cylinders 2 and 4] and AEH 644 [for cylinders 1 and 3]); with these go connecting rod bearings (Part No. AEH 434 [half]). When using these bearings and the standard main bearings, neither of which has racing clearances, it is necessary to run in steadily for 30 hours on the test stand or for 1,000 road miles (1600 km.). Do not apply full power at an early stage, but wait until the bearings bed down, and develop a good running condition without temperature rise.

If you wish to put your engine on to full power early, then see note reference bearings with initial racing clearances on page 28.

To increase the oil pressure fit a packing piece in the end of the oil release valve cap behind the release valve spring; this should be ·200 in. (5·08 mm.) thick by $\frac{31}{64}$ in. (12·3 mm.) dia. or two packings ·100 in. (2·54 mm.) thick (Part No. AEH 798). See page 40 for further details on oil pump and filter bottle top.

Fit the competition clutch (see page 28). See page 30 for reference to the flywheel.

Fit the large 1¾ in. (44·45 mm.) S.U. carburetter as in Stage 3.

Use the special distributor (Part No. BHA 4415) (see page 34), which has a suitable automatic advance and no vacuum advance. The static setting should be 6° B.T.D.C. and not more than 8° nor less than 5°. If this distributor is not available a nearly similar one (Part No. AEJ 41), distributor No. 40718A, is generally suitable, but this must be set 2° B.T.D.C. and not more than 4° nor less than 1°. The standard distributor (for H.C. engines), which is Part No. 12H 792, distributor No. 40897, is not quite so suitable, but if it was desired to use it, then it should be set 9° to 11° B.T.D.C.

Sparking plugs should be Champion N58R, but, according to the circuit you may be able to use Champion N63R or N3.

Use 100 (minimum) octane fuel.

The engine should develop the following brake-horse-power:

R.p.m.	B.h.p.
3,000	62
4,000	89
5,000	111
5,500	120
6,000	121
6,500	119

Stage 5
9·3 to 9·5 : 1 compression ratio (Weber carburetter)

Prepare your engine as Stage 4, but in place of the S.U. 1¾ in. (44·45 mm.) carburetters, fit a 45 DCOE 13 Weber twin-choke carburetter. This will require a special inlet manifold and parts as detailed on pages 46 and 47. See page 30 for particulars of settings.

There is only a marginal improvement to be gained by the fitting of the Weber carburetters, with some slight loss at the lower r.p.m., but some drivers prefer this type of carburetter.

The carburetters are mounted on synthetic rubber 'O' ring gaskets to prevent vibration of the carburetter mechanism and disturbance of the fuel-to-air ratio. Under each carburetter fixing nut a double-coil spring washer (Part No. AJD 7732) should be fitted; each fixing nut should be drilled and wired in pairs to prevent them coming slack. Tighten the nuts up fairly firmly, but by gripping the carburetter some slight free movement should be felt.

Steady rods are fitted from the inlet manifold, both front and rear, down to brackets on the cylinder block; adjust these rods to the free position so that the bolts go easily through the fork ends and brackets, tighten the bolts solid, and lock up the fork locknuts.

The engine, using 100 (minimum) octane fuel, should give the following power output:

	R.p.m.	B.h.p.	Gal. per hr. fuel consumption	
			Imperial	U.S.
B.h.p. taken at gearbox tail flange	3,000	63·5	4·3	5·2
	3,500	78	5·4	6·5
	4,000	92·5	6·0	7·2
	4,500	106·5	6·6	7·9
	5,000	114	7·1	8·5
	5,500	121	7·5	9·0
	6,000	122	8·4	10·0
	6,500	121	9·0	10·8

For bench testing use Champion N58R plugs, but on the circuit you may be able to use softer plugs. If the circuit is short you may find N3 in cylinders 1 and 4, and N63R in cylinders 2 and 3 will be suitable.

If the circuit is long you may require N63R in cylinders 1 and 4 and N58R in cylinders 2 and 3. The centre cylinders are inclined to run hotter due to the proximity of the two exhaust valves.

TUNING

Stage 6
10·4 to 10·6 : 1 compression ratio (competition tuning)

Tune as for Stage 4, or Stage 5, but remove $\frac{1}{16}$ in. (1·59 mm.) from the cylinder head face, making the thickness of the head $3\frac{7}{64} \pm \cdot015$ in. (79 $\pm \cdot38$ mm.). The standard thickness of the cylinder head is $3\frac{11}{64} {}^{+\cdot015}_{-\cdot000}$ in. (80·6 ${}^{+\cdot38}_{-\cdot00}$ mm.). Finally surface grind the face of the head and carefully lap as described on page 26.

Check the opening of the exhaust valves at full lift to ensure they have a minimum of $\frac{1}{16}$ in. (1·59 mm.) over-travel; if not, the undercut in the block face will have to be increased the required amount.

Use Champion N58R sparking plugs.

The engine should give the following power output on 100 (minimum) octane fuel.

	R.p.m.	B.h.p. on S.U. 1¼ in. Carb. (Two)	B.h.p. on Weber Carburetter 45 DCOE 13	B.h.p. on Weber with 38 choke 175 main 160 air corrected
B.h.p. taken at gearbox tail flange	3,000	64	65	64
	3,500	76	82	81
	4,000	91	96	95
	4,500	106	109	108
	5,000	114·5	120	120
	5,500	126	128	127·5
	6,000	128·5	130	131
	6,500	129	127	128

Note.—While using 100-octane fuel and the camshaft as listed for Stage 4, no worthwhile power increase will be gained by further raising of the compression ratio.

OTHER SPECIAL ITEMS

Brakes

After many consecutive applications of the brakes during competition driving some brake fade may be experienced with the standard linings. Competition front disc pads and rear brake-shoe linings or lined shoes are available (see list). The rear linings are made to a thickness suitable for grinding to radius after fitment. The front pads are of a suitable heavy-duty material. With fair competition driving these linings will be free from fade, but will give a harder pedal effort on application.

When the lining friction value is altered from that of the standard car it may be found that changing the rear wheel cylinders to ones of smaller size ($\frac{3}{4}$ in. [19·05 mm.] dia.) will improve the front to rear brake ratio.

As these wheel cylinders have a dowel on the fitting face, it will be necessary to drill a hole in the back plate to match this dowel.

Braze a steel plug in the existing hole and face off level with the plate before drilling the new hole. The size of the hole is ·170 to ·175 in. (4·32 to 4·45 mm.) dia. and drilled ·578 in. (14·68 mm.) above the centre of the cylinder mounting hole and ·350 in. (8·89 mm.) offset from the radial centre-line of the cylinder mounting hole.

When using your car on a racing circuit always remove the dust shields from the front disc brakes. This will enable the discs and brakes to run at a lower temperature and will decrease the possibility of brake fade.

Balancing of road wheel and tyre assemblies

To obtain the smoothest steering, free from all steering-wheel kick, and to eliminate any tendency to front-wheel patter, especially at speeds around 70 m.p.h. (113 km./h.) and over, it will be found beneficial to have the front road wheel and tyre assemblies statically and dynamically balanced. This usually results in balance weights being fitted on both sides of the rims, but this dynamic balancing is well worth while. Balance may require re-checking every few thousand miles if the car suffers brake locking, etc., as this may again put the tyres out of balance enough for the effect to be felt.

It is advisable to keep front tyres in good condition and free from uneven tread wear. This can sometimes be done by changing tyres from front to rear before uneven wear develops. Pick the best tyres for use at the front (or those that have even tread wear and run true) before they are dynamically balanced. Balancing a tyre which has flats or uneven wear is not usually very successful. In some cases the tread can be buffed true, but this is not an economic way of using rubber.

Valves and guides

The valves fitted as standard are of high quality, but if valves are desired with a longer service life or increased resistance to burning special valves are available in Nimonic alloy—inlet (Part No. AEH 757) and exhaust (Part No. AEH 758). (See list.) These must be used in conjunction with special spring collars (Part No. AEH 760) and also special cotters (Part No. AEH 761) to suit the half-round groove in the valve stem. If triple valve springs are used, top collar (Part No. AHH 7313) must be used. These valves should be used in conjunction with bronze (Hidural 5) guides for both the inlet and exhaust valves, inlet (Part No. AEH 755) and exhaust (Part No. AEH 756). The inlet guide is $2\frac{1}{16}$ in. (27 mm.) long and the exhaust $2\frac{5}{16}$ in. (33·4 mm.) long. They should be pressed into the head so that they are left standing out between $\frac{49}{64}$ and $\frac{50}{64}$ in. (19·4 and 19·8 mm.).

OTHER SPECIAL ITEMS

Cylinder head gasket

When the compression is raised it may be necessary to use a reinforced gasket. A competition cylinder head gasket is available (see list) constructed from ·009 in. copper and steel with internal reinforcements (Part No. AEH 768). As the cylinder block and head faces may suffer some distortion in the early life of the engine it is advisable to check these faces for flatness before fitting the new gasket. If the faces are distorted they should be finely surface ground, and a certain amount of careful lapping or flat scraping is worth while. Do not lap excessively as this will only produce an uneven surface. Check them finally together with marking.

Before replacing the cylinder head studs slightly countersink (not too heavily) the tops of the threaded holes in the cylinder block. This will enable the head to pull down around the studs and seal more efficiently.

To maintain the clamping pressure of the cylinder head onto the gasket it is advantageous to remove the flat washers under the 11 cylinder head nuts and replace these with more rigid ones of $\frac{3}{32}$ in. (2·4 mm.) thickness by $\frac{3}{4}$ in. (19 mm.) outside diameter and with a hole ·390 in. (9·91 mm.) dia. These can be turned up from a 40-ton steel bar, or if made from mild steel they should be case-hardened.

Valve springs

The valve bounce r.p.m. on the standard engine is 6,230 r.p.m. and the valve springs, operating mechanism, and drive are safely stressed to maintain this.

If for very special competition purposes it is desired to raise the valve bounce period, the appropriate springs may be selected from the following table:

Part No. outer springs	lb.	Part No. inner springs	lb.	Total lb. full lift	Valve bounce r.p.m.		
					Standard camshaft	Comp. camshaft AEH 714	Comp. camshaft AEH 770
1H 1111*	117	1H 723*	50	167	6,230	6,500	6,500
1H 1111	117	1H 1112	57	174	6,360	6,600	6,600
AHH 7264	131	1H 723	50	181	6,480	6,700	6,700
AHH 7264	131	1H 1112	57	188	6,600	6,750	6,750
AHH 7264	131	AHH 7265	60	210	6,680	6,800	6,800

* Standard engine.

It is advised that these springs be used only for very special events, as if used under everyday conditions the cams and followers will have a shorter service life. The springs will not necessarily give an increase in brake-horse-power, but will extend the same horse-power up to valve bounce. This is sometimes useful in enabling a lower gear to be retained, still maintaining the same maximum speed, with increased power for acceleration.

As an absolute maximum, triple valves springs (Part No. AHH 7309) may be used, in conjunction with a special valve spring top collar (Part No. AHH 7313). No bottom collar is used, but the counterbore around the valve guide in the head face must be increased to 1,520 to 1·515 in. (3·86 to 3·85 mm.) dia. The springs are supplied, tightly nested in sets of three, giving a total full lift load of 230 lb. (104·3 kg.).

The valve crash position will be above 7,000 r.p.m.

OTHER SPECIAL ITEMS

Rear axle ratios

With the combination of the 4·55, 4·3, 4·1, and 3·9 : 1 axle ratios available and the standard and close-ratio gears it is possible to obtain a combination of conditions suitable for most competition purposes.

Close-ratio gearbox

Close-ratio gears are available giving gearbox ratios of—third 1·268 : 1, second 1·62 : 1, first 2·45 : 1.

The following parts are required:

	Part No.		No. off
	22H 464	Laygear	1
	22H 465	Layshaft	1
	22H 466	Thrust washer (for laygear front)	1
	22H 467		
Alternatives {	22H 468 22H 469 22H 470 }	Thrust washer (for laygear rear)	1
	22H 471	Caged needle-roller bearing (17 × 23 × 15) mm.	4
	22H 472	First motion shaft	1
	1H 3299	Second speed mainshaft gear ..	1
	1H 3300	Third speed mainshaft gear ..	1

An additional roller bearing has been added to the layshaft for load carrying; there are now two rollers at each end of the shaft. The rollers are a different type to standard, so four roller bearings will be required.

The layshaft 22H 465 is larger than the standard one, and this will necessitate the reboring of the holes in the gearbox casing in which the layshaft is mounted. These should be fine-bored and reamed in line to ·6688/·6699 in. in diameter. Get a capable machinist to do this work.

As an alternative to the foregoing, you may have available the close-ratio gears for the 'MGA'. (These are the same numerical ratio.)

Part No.		No. off
1H 3297	First motion shaft	1
1H 3298	Laygear	1
1H 3299	Second speed mainshaft gear ..	1
1H 3300	Third speed mainshaft gear ..	1

These can be fitted to the 'MGB' gearbox casing, but as the splines on the 'MGA' input shaft are wide and the ones on the 'MGB' are fine, it is necessary to use the 'MGA' Twin Cam centre plate (Part No. 27H 3241).

Water thermostat and fan

For sustained maximum power and speed, such as in road-racing conditions, it is advantageous to remove the thermostat. This will ensure the maximum water flow. In place of the thermostat fit the blanking sleeve (thermostat by-pass) (see list, page 43).

The fan should also be removed and the bolts refitted with flat washers.

OTHER SPECIAL ITEMS

Oil cooler

An aluminium-alloy oil cooler is available. This can be supplied together with high-duty flexible hoses, hose grommets, hose straps, unions, and gaskets, and can easily be mounted on the floor behind the radiator grille as depicted in Fig. 1 (see Spare Parts List for details).

Fuel pump

Check the fuel flow of your petrol pump by removing the two float-chamber tops complete with the fuel lines. Unclip the main fuel line and reassemble it alongside the car so that the two float-chamber tops (complete with needles and levers) can be held over a 2-gal. (2·4 U.S. gal., 9·1-litre), or larger can. Switch on the pump and check the time for 1 gal. (9·6 U.S. pints, 4·55 litres) to flow. The standard engine uses a maximum of approx. 7·2 gal. (8·6 U.S. gal., 32·76 litres) an hour, and the engine tuned to Stage 6 uses approximately 9 gal. (10·8 U.S. gal., 40·95 litres) an hour. A good pump may flow at 13 gal. (15·6 U.S. gal., 59·15 litres) an hour, but a pump needing attention may only flow at 6 gal. (7·2 U.S. gal., 27·3 litres) an hour.

If a pump is required which will give a flow with a wide safety margin S.U. fuel pump (Part No. AUA 173) is available. The mounting bracket will need slight alteration to mount this pump and the fuel lines reset to suit. Alternatively two standard fuel pumps could be used.

Clutch

With increased power output a competition clutch having more torque capacity, etc., may be required (see page 44 for details). This clutch assembly has a stronger diaphragm spring, and a driven plate with riveted and bonded linings. It is desirable to ventilate the clutch pit for competition purposes. This may be done by removing the drain split pin in the base of the bell housing and drilling the hole out to $\frac{5}{8}$ in. (15·9 mm.) dia. Discard the rubber bellows from the clutch operating lever. Drill a hole 1¼ in. (31·7 mm.) dia. at the top centre of the bell housing (3 in. [76·2 mm.] down from the bolting flange) and make up and fit a 22 S.W.G. sheet-metal square box cover over this hole 2 in. × 2 in. × $\frac{5}{8}$ in. (50·8 mm. × 50·8 mm. × 15·9 mm.) deep with an open end $\frac{5}{8}$ in. × 2 in. (15·9 mm. × 50·8 mm.) towards the clutch lever side of the gearbox and the top, bottom, and other end closed in. A flange $\frac{3}{8}$ in. (9·5 mm.) wide can be made top and bottom to fix the cover to the bell housing with four $\frac{1}{8}$ in. (3·2 mm.) dia. rivets.

Crankshaft bearings

The standard main and big-end bearings have suitable close clearances for the quietness of the running of the standard engine. When using the engine for racing purposes, especially above 6,000 r.p.m., it is desirable to use both main and big-end bearings with increased initial clearances. The standard bearings are of lead-indium type. The increased clearance bearings of the lead-indium type are: main bearings (set of six halves), Part No. 8G 8843 (bearing stamped V.P.4769), and big-end bearings (half), Part No. AEH 434 or set of eight halves, Part No. 8G 2259.

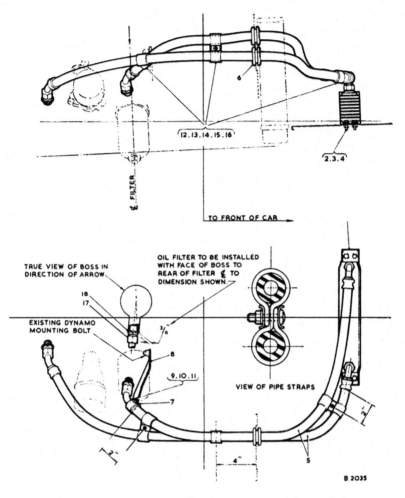

Fig. 1

The oil cooler general arrangement

1.	Oil cooler.	
2.	Screws—cooler to front apron.	
3.	Washers—plain—for screws.	
4.	Washers—spring—for screws.	
5.	Flexible pipes.	
6.	Grommets.	
7.	Clip—flexible pipe.	
8.	Strap—support.	
9.	Screw—clip to support strap.	
10.	Washer—spring—for clip.	
11.	Nut for clip.	
12.	Clips—strap (rubber).	
13.	Plates—clamp—for strap clip.	
14.	Screws for clamp plate.	
15.	Washers—spring—for clamp plate.	
16.	Nuts for clamp plates.	
17.	Union adaptor.	
18.	Washer—union adaptor.	

OTHER SPECIAL ITEMS

Weber carburetters (45 DCOE 13)

These will require a special inlet manifold and parts as detailed on pages 46 and 47. (See Figs. 2 and 3 for installation details.)

The carburetters are mounted on synthetic rubber 'O' ring gaskets to prevent vibration of the carburetter mechanism and disturbance of the fuel-to-air ratio.

Under each carburetter fixing nut a double-coil spring washer (Part No. AJD 7732) should be fitted; each fixing nut should be drilled and wired in pairs to prevent them coming slack. Tighten the nuts up fairly firmly, but by gripping the carburetter some slight free movement should be felt.

Steady rods are fitted from the inlet manifold, both front and rear, down to brackets on the cylinder block; adjust these rods to the free position so that the bolts go easily through the fork ends and brackets. Tighten the bolts solid and lock up the fork locknuts. (See Fig. 3 for details.)

The settings supplied in the carburetters should be as below:

Auxiliary venturi	5·000 mm.
Chokes	36 mm.
Main jet	1·70 mm.
Air correction jet	1·60 mm.
Emulsion tubes	F16
Idling jets	·60/F8
Pump jets	·60

Needle valve 2·25 mm. must be spring-loaded type.

Level between the float and cover gasket to be 5 mm.

The pump inlet valve should have a hole of 2·00 mm. in the top and an exhaust hole in the side of 1·00 mm. dia.

These settings should be found correct for Stage 5 onwards.

For endurance running in long-distance races a richer 175 main is beneficial.

The spring-loaded needle valve prevents mixture variation due to vibration.

If the pick-up condition can be tolerated, the power can be slightly increased at the top end by fitting 38 mm. chokes and 175 main jets with a 160 air jet; again for long distance a 180 or 185 main used with a 160 air jet will maintain performance, but note that it slightly decreases the power at the lower range.

It is sometimes found that to use a 3·5 auxiliary venturi in place of the 5·00 will give improved pick-up conditions, but this is a matter of trial under the local conditions.

Crankshaft

The standard crankshaft is quite satisfactory, but with continued high duty in due course will show some wear, and may need renewing at intervals. It may be cheaper to renew the standard shaft at suitable intervals. If required, an induction-hardened and heavy-duty crankshaft can be used (see list, page 45).

Flywheel

The standard flywheel is in high-grade cast iron; if a steel flywheel is preferred see the list for the part number.

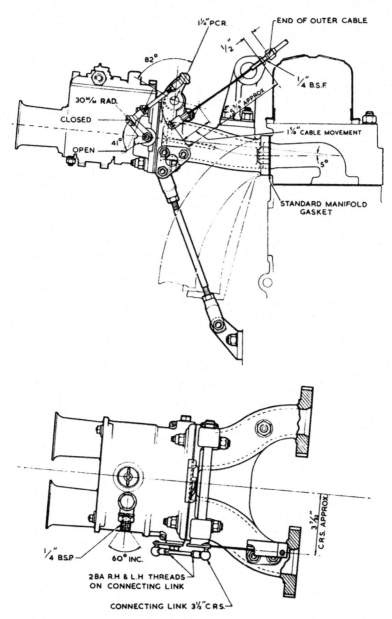

Fig. 2
Weber carburetter installation details

B.2014

OTHER SPECIAL ITEMS

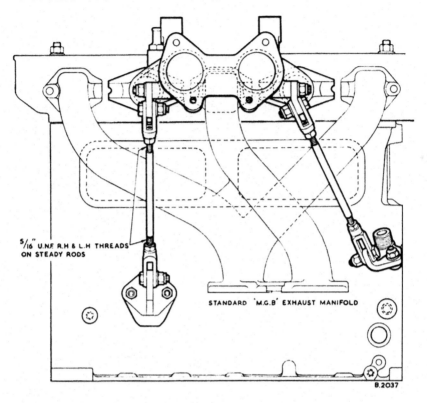

5/16" U.N.F. R.H & L.H THREADS
ON STEADY RODS

STANDARD 'M.G.B' EXHAUST MANIFOLD

B.2037

Fig. 3
Weber carburetter—steady rods arrangement

OTHER SPECIAL ITEMS

Timing chain sprockets

With high r.p.m. and the use of high-lift camshafts the sprockets have to withstand a much heavier duty. The standard sprockets are cast iron, but steel sprockets for both crankshaft and camshaft are listed on page 45.

Road springs

The standard car is arranged with a good combination of control and ride comfort for all conditions of road surface.

For competition purposes and optimum balance of weight transfer on corners the best condition should be:

A. Competition roll bar ⅝ in. (15·9 mm.) dia.

B. Front coil springs (100 lb./in. [1·15 kg./m.] rate at wheel).

C. Rear springs (93 lb./in. [1·075 kg./m.] rate at wheel)—Part No. AHH 7080.

D. Short rear bump rubbers (Part No. AHH 7074).

See list on page 43 for the competition front coil springs of 100 lb./in. rate at the wheel.

The standard coil springs are 73 lb./in. (·842 kg./m.) rate at the wheel.

The rear springs (now standard) (Part No. AHH 7080) may already be on your car; these can be recognized by the fact that they have plastic interleaving between the leaves, and the leaf clips (six in number) have rubber bands under them. It comprises two top leaves at $\frac{7}{32}$ in. (5·6 mm.) with three leaves of $\frac{3}{16}$ in. (4·8 mm.) and bottom plate $\frac{7}{32}$ in. (5·6 mm.) thick.

The original rear spring of 99 lb./in. rate at the wheel has no interleaving, has plain steel clips, and comprises five leaves $\frac{7}{32}$ in. (5·6 mm.) thick and bottom plate of $\frac{7}{32}$ in. (5·6 mm.) thick.

You can recognize the short rear bump rubber by its $2\frac{5}{32}$ in. (54·8 mm.) outside dia. and $2\frac{5}{32}$ in. (54·8 mm.) length.

Note.—The ⅝ in. (15·9 mm.) roll bar may give some harshness on the front end but is satisfactory for competition purposes. If desired, the production optional extra $\frac{9}{16}$ in. (14·3 mm.) dia. roll bar can be used, and the cornering will only be slightly affected.

The condition (A, B, C, D) will give a certain amount of roll angle; this is perfectly in order, but if a lesser angle and harder ride are preferred, the 99 lb./in. (1·144 kg./m.) rear springs (Part No. AHH 6453) may be used in conjunction with the 100 lb./in. (1·15 kg./m.) front coil springs and using the ⅝ in. (15·9 mm.) dia. front anti-roll bar and its two ⅝ in. (15·9 mm.) dia. rubber mountings. The cornering speed is not quite so high, but the feeling of stability may suit the driver.

Shock absorbers

Shock absorbers with higher settings may be used for competition work if a firm control is desired, but some drivers may prefer the standard settings.

Your standard shock absorbers can be converted by fitting the high setting valves only (see list for details, page 43).

OTHER SPECIAL ITEMS

Distributor

The special distributor used in Stage 4 has no vacuum advance and has an advance curve as illustrated in Fig. 4.

The part number is BHA 4415 and the distributor number 40943A (with 32-oz. springs).

The automatic advance in crankshaft degrees is 24° and with a static setting of, say, 6° crankshaft degrees B.T.D.C. gives a maximum advance of 30°.

If this distributor is not available, the 'MGA' Twin Cam distributor is a near alternative (Part No. AEJ 41). This has an automatic advance of 28°, so, with the static setting of, say, 2° crankshaft degrees B.T.D.C., will also give a maximum advance of 30°. The advance curve will not be very far out.

Sparking plugs

The standard plug was Champion N5, but is now N–9Y. For competition purposes N3 is recommended, or if a colder grade of plug is required use N63R, or colder N58R.

Dynamo

For long-distance races it is preferable to run the dynamo at a slower speed by the fitting of a suitable pulley and drive belt (see list for details, page 46).

Exhaust system

The twin exhaust header and down pipes are an efficient arrangement and cannot be improved significantly, except from the weight angle.

For competition purposes the system could be made more durable and cooler running by removing the centre silencer and replacing this with a plain pipe of 2 in. (50·8 mm.) outside diameter and approximately ·048 in. (1·22 mm.) thick, extending from the 'V' junction of the twin pipes up to the rear position of the centre silencer. Alter the end of the 'V' junction to match the 2 in. (50·8 mm.) pipe.

The tail pipe and rear silencer should be retained.

If a lightweight steel tube exhaust header is desired, one is available (see details on page 46).

The noise level will, of course, be increased (see 'FOREWORD' regarding regulations).

Fly-off hand brake

If you wish to convert your hand brake to the fly-off type, all you require is a new reversed pawl and a pawl operating rod (see details on page 43).

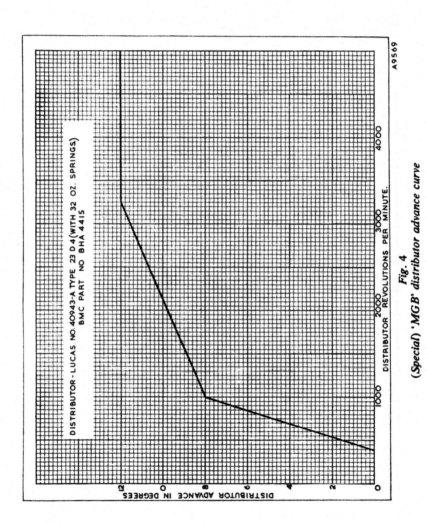

A9569

Fig. 4
(Special) 'MGB' distributor advance curve

OTHER SPECIAL ITEMS

Engine oil sump

Especially in long-distance racing, the oil level may drop to a position where oil surge on violent cornering and braking may cause a temporary but complete loss of oil pressure. This could be seriously detrimental to the engine and may result in bearing failure. It is advisable to increase the oil capacity above the oil pump inlet and to fit a baffle in the oil sump to prevent the oil surging away from the pump inlet. This can be done by fitting the deep sump or altering your own sump by cutting through approximately 1¼ in. (31·7 mm.) from the bottom and gas welding in a 1-in. (25·4 mm.) distance piece of sheet metal, or obtaining another sump and cutting off 2¼ in. (57·1 mm.) from the bottom and welding this to the top of your sump.

Make up and spot-weld the surge baffle to the inside of the oil sump as illustrated in Figs. 5 and 6.

Fit the 1-in. (25·4 mm.) packing piece between the pump strainer and pump extension (Part No. AHH 7238), using an extra gasket and 1 in. (25·4 mm.) longer bolts. This will lower the oil pick-up to the correct position.

Weld an extension piece 1 in. (25·4 mm.) long onto the end of your oil dipstick so that the original oil level is maintained, or use the stick as it is, and make a new maximum high-level mark 1 in. (25·4 mm.) above the existing one.

For short circuits, where oil levels may not drop, the standard depth of sump should be found satisfactory, but the surge baffle should be made up and fitted as illustrated.

Gearbox dipstick and oil seal

To ensure that no oil leaks occur from the gearbox during the arduous conditions of competition work you can fit a gearbox dipstick (Part No. AEC 3683) which is retained by rubber sealing rings.

The one listed will need alteration by cutting off 2 7/16 in. (61·9 mm.) and re-marking 'HIGH' and 'LOW' levels (as old dipstick); this will then make it suitable for the 'MGB' gearbox.

Also ascertain if the front gearbox cover is fitted with a high-duty mainshaft oil seal (Part No. 22H 475); at the same time check the front gear box cover (in which the seal is mounted) for perfect flatness and refit with jointing compound. This will ensure that no gearbox oil will get through onto the clutch facings.

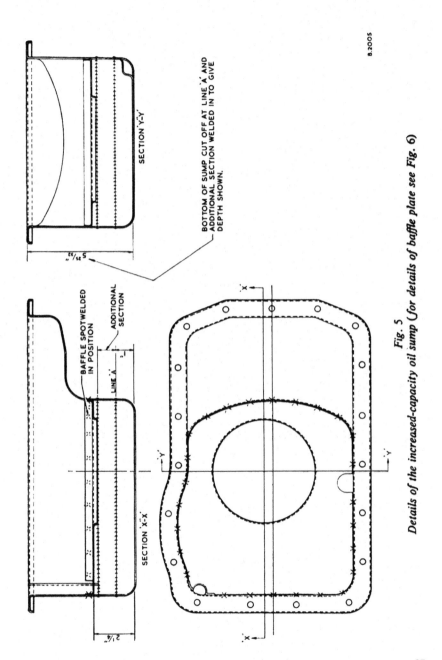

B.2005

SECTION 'Y-Y'

BOTTOM OF SUMP CUT OFF AT LINE 'A' AND
ADDITIONAL SECTION WELDED IN TO GIVE
DEPTH SHOWN.

5 $^{25}/_{32}$"

BAFFLE SPOT WELDED
IN POSITION

ADDITIONAL
SECTION

LINE 'A'

SECTION 'X-X'

2 $^{1}/_{8}$"

Fig. 5

Details of the increased-capacity oil sump (for details of baffle plate see Fig. 6)

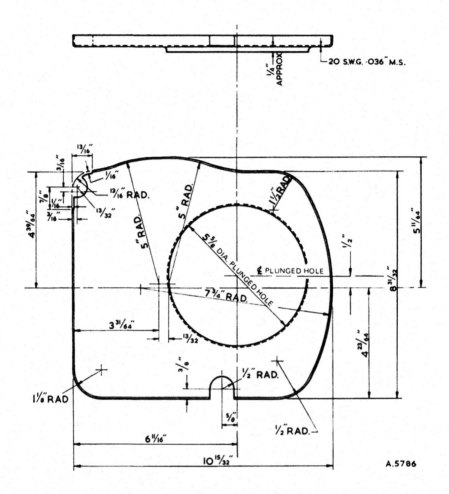

Fig. 6
Detail of oil sump baffle plate

OTHER SPECIAL ITEMS

Fuel tank supplementary (total capacity 20 gal. [24·2 U.S. gal., 90·92 litres])

This fuel tank of 10 gal. (12·1 U.S. gal., 45·5 litres) capacity is fitted in the trunk on supports similar to those on the under side of the trunk floor supporting the standard tank. These supports are bolted at intervals to the swages in the trunk floor.

Connections are made through flanged holes cut in the floor to a modified standard tank using rubber hose and eight hose clips. A seal must be made between the trunk floor and the bottom tank at the points at which the connectors pass through the floor.

The filler tube is brought through the hole in the trunk lid on the right-hand side, using a suitable seal between the filler neck surround and the trunk lid.

The spare wheel is strapped across the supplementary tank, using a leather strap diagonally between the rear floor panel and the trunk floor outer (left-hand side). The following is a list of parts (only available to special order):

Part No.		No. off
A 7174 X	Trunk floor arrangement	Ref.
SK 7428 X	Sketch showing modification to trunk floor ..	Ref.
AHH 7094	Tank support—trunk floor	2
PMZ 0306	No. 10 UNF. pan head screws	18
LWZ 303	No. 10 (·190) spring washers	18
FNZ 103	No. 10 UNF. nuts	18
AHH 7239	Assembly of 20-gal. (24·2 U.S. gal., 90·92 litres) fuel tanks complete. (Drawing)	Ref.
AHH 7050	Supplementary tank 10 gal. (12·1 U.S. gal., 45·5 litres) capacity	1
AHH 7051	10-gal. (12·1 U.S. gal., 45·5 litres) fuel tank (modified standard)	1
AHH 7243	Seal—small—bottom tank to floor	1
AHH 7244	Seal—large—bottom tank to floor	1
AHH 7093	Rubber connecting hose	2
HCS 1622	Connecting hose clips	4
AHH 6253	Tank straps	2
AHH 6257	Rear hanger	2
AHH 6252	Packing strip—tank strap to tank	2
CLZ 0427	Clevis pin	4
PWZ 104	Plain washer	4
ZPS 0205	Split pin	4
HBZ 0418	¼ in. UNF. hexagon head bolt	2
PWZ 104	¼ in. plain washer	2
LNZ 104	¼ in. UNF. stiffnut	2
SK 7427 Y	Sketch showing hole in trunk lid	Ref.
AHH 7241	Filler neck surround	1
HCS 1622	Pipe clip—filler surround to filler neck ..	1
AHH 7245	Seal—trunk lid to filler neck surround	1
AHH 7240	Quick-release filler cap (B1685D—Enots) (2½ in. [63·5 mm.] outside dia. pipe fitting)	1
AHH 7242	Spare wheel—strap and staple assembly ..	1
PMZ 0306	No. 10 UNF. pan head screws	4
LWZ 303	No. 10 (·190) spring washers	4
FNZ 103	No. 10 UNF. nuts	4

OTHER SPECIAL ITEMS

Oil pump

The oil pressure may be increased by packing the oil relief valve springs; this is done by fitting a circular steel packing of ⅝ in. (12·3 mm.) dia. in the end of the release valve cap and behind the relief valve spring. These packings may be of ·100, ·200, ·300, or ·400 in. (2·54, 5·08, 7·62, or 10·16 mm.) thick, or multiples of the ·100 in. (2·54 mm.) packing can be used.

Under the cap two fibre gaskets are also fitted; one of these can be removed, or, better, both removed and replaced with one thin copper gasket (Part No. 6K 431).

Between 70 and 80 lb./sq. in. (4·92 and 5·62 kg./cm.^{2}) and up to 100 lb./sq. in. (7·03 kg./cm.^{2}) is a good pressure and dropping to 30/40 lb./sq. in. (2·11/2·81 kg./cm.^{2}) is satisfactory.

It is sometimes found that the oil pressure increases up to, say, 5,500 r.p.m. and drops off in pressure beyond this speed. This can be prevented by machining the pump cover and making twin inlet ports to the pump. (See Fig. 7 for machining.)

A point which should be carefully checked is the oil pump strainer. The threaded attachment plate is spot-welded to the inside face of the strainer top plate. If the strainer top plate is not flat, or if the attachment plate has not pulled up perfectly to the under side of the top plate, an air leak can occur between the attachment plate and the top plate. Ensure that the top plate is flat over the gasket area, and to make sure that no air leak can occur carefully warm the whole strainer up and tin around the hole in the top plate to the attachment plate so that the bottom corner joint is sealed. Under normal conditions this position is under oil level, but when oil surge occurs, as in competition work, it may become uncovered.

Oil filter

It is not essential, but it gives some slight improvement in the oil flow, to machine an undercut in the face of the top casting of the filter bottle; this allows an unrestricted flow of oil from the square feed hole. (See Fig. 8 for details.) You must remove the circular plate from the casting to do this; lever the plate off carefully, and ensure that it is flat before replacing and peening over.

Torque wrench settings

When tightening the cylinder head nuts to 50 ft. lb. (6·91 m. kg.) ensure that they are correctly and evenly tightened.

The main bearing nuts should be tightened to 70/75 ft. lb. (9·68/10·37 m. kg.).

Big-end bolts should be tightened carefully to 40/45 ft. lb. (5·53/6·22 m. kg.) only; overtightening to more than 45 ft. lb. (6·22 m. kg.) will only cause fracture of the bolts in operation.

Tighten the flywheel bolts to 40 ft. lb. (5·53 m. kg.).

Tighten the gudgeon pin bolts to 25 ft. lb. (3·46 m. kg.) and clutch bolts to 25/30 ft. lb. (3·46/4·15 m. kg.).

OTHER SPECIAL ITEMS

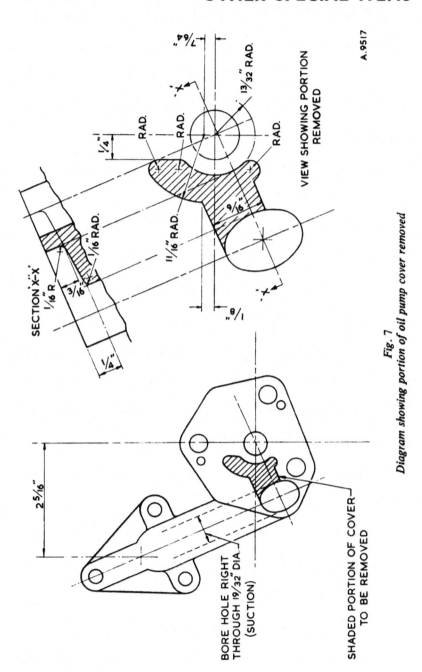

Fig. 7
Diagram showing portion of oil pump cover removed

41

OTHER SPECIAL ITEMS

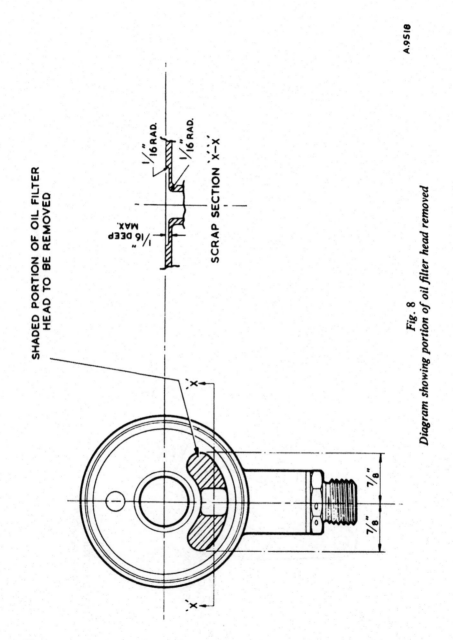

Fig. 8
Diagram showing portion of oil filter head removed

COMPETITION EQUIPMENT

General

	Part No.	No. off
Steering-wheel (wood-rimmed, light alloy)	AHH 7208	1
Carburetters—1¾ in. (44·45 mm.), 1 pair S.U.	AUC 780	1
Extension flare pipe for 1¾ in. S.U. carburetter—rear..	AHH 7209	1
Extension flare pipe for 1¾ in. S.U. carburetter—front	AHH 7219	1
Gasket—carburetter—for 1¾ in. S.U. carburetter ..	AHH 5791	1
Inlet manifold for 1¾ in. S.U. carburetter	AEH 200	1
Valve springs—inner	1H 1112	8
Crown wheel and pinion (10/41)—4·1 : 1 ratio ..	ATB 7240	1
Speedometer for 4·1 : 1 ratio rear axle— m.p.h.	To special order	—	1
Speedometer for 4·1 : 1 ratio rear axle— km.p.h.		—	1
Crown wheel and pinion (9/41)—4·55 : 1 ratio ..	BTB 57	1
Speedometer for 4·55 : 1 ratio rear axle— m.p.h.	To special order	—	1
Speedometer for 4·55 : 1 ratio rear axle— km.p.h.		—	1
Crown wheel and pinion (10/43)—4·3 : 1 ratio ..	BTB 323	1
Speedometer for 4·3 : 1 ratio rear axle— m.p.h.	To special order	—	1
Speedometer for 4·3 : 1 ratio rear axle— km.p.h.		—	1
Blanking sleeve (thermostat by-pass)	11G 176	1

Brakes

	Part No.	No. off
Brake pads (set 4) (Ferodo D.S.11)—competition facings	8G 8834	1
Rear brake-shoe and lining assembly (set 2) (Ferodo V.G.95/1) (competition facings)	8G 8828	1
Rear brake lining (with rivets) (set 4) (Ferodo V.G. 95/1) (competition facings)	8G 8829	1
Rear wheel brake cylinder assembly—¾ in. (19 mm.) dia.	17H 8152	2
Pawl hand brake lever (for fly-off hand brake) ..	AHH 7223	1
Pawl rod (for fly-off hand brake)	AHH 7222	1
Servo brake (kit)	8G 8732	1

Suspension

	Part No.	No. off
Shock absorbers (competition setting)—front.. ..	AHH 7104	
Shock absorbers (competition setting)—rear R.H. ..	AHH 7105	
Shock absorbers (competition setting)—rear L.H. ..	AHH 7106	As required
Shock absorber valve assembly (only) (competition setting)—front	AHH 7217	
Shock absorber valve assembly (only) (competition setting)—rear	AHH 7218	
Front coil springs (100 lb. [45·4 kg.] at wheel) ..	AHH 5789	2

COMPETITION EQUIPMENT

Suspension—*continued*	Part No.	No. off
Optional extra anti-roll bar—$\frac{9}{16}$ in. (14·3 mm.) dia. ..	AHH 7329	1

		Part No.	No. off
	Link—anti-roll bar—R.H.	AHH 6543	1
	Link—anti-roll bar—L.H.	AHH 6544	1
	Bearing—anti-roll bar	AHH 6541	2
	Bearing strap	1B 7356	2
	Clamping bolt	AHH 5941	2
	$\frac{5}{16}$ in. dia. plain washer	PWZ 107	2
	$\frac{5}{16}$ in. UNF. Aerotight nut ..	LNZ 107	2
Parts for	$\frac{5}{16}$ in. UNF. × $\frac{5}{8}$ in. hexagon head screw ..	HZS 0505	4
anti-roll	$\frac{5}{16}$ in. dia. spring washer	LWZ 205	4
bar	$\frac{1}{2}$ in. dia. spring washer	LWZ 208	2
	$\frac{1}{2}$ in. UNF. hexagon head nut	FNZ 108	2
	End location stop	AHH 6546	4
	No. 10 recessed pan head screw	PMZ 0308	4
	Spring washer	LWZ 203	4
	Nut	FNZ 103	4
	Bottom wishbone assembly—R.H. ..	AHH 5927	1
	Bottom wishbone assembly—L.H. ..	AHH 5929	1
Alternative $\frac{5}{8}$ in. dia. anti-roll bar		AHH 7331	1
Bearing for $\frac{5}{8}$ in. anti-roll bar		1B 4526	2

Close-ratio gears

		Part No.	No. off
	Gearbox assembly (with remote control)—		
	non-overdrive	22H 461	1
	Gearbox assembly (with remote control)—		
	with overdrive	22H 462	1
3rd	Including:		
1·268 : 1	Gearbox casing assembly (overdrive) ..	48G 314	1
	Gearbox casing assembly (non-overdrive)	48G 315	1
2nd	Laygear	22H 464	1
1·62 : 1	Layshaft	22H 465	1
	Thrust washer for laygear (front) ..	22H 466	1
1st	Thrust washer for laygear (rear) (or		
2·45 : 1	22H 468, 469, or 470)..	22H 467	1
	Caged needle-roller bearing (for laygear)	22H 471	4
	First motion shaft	22H 472	1
	Second speed mainshaft gear	1H 3299	1
	Third speed mainshaft gear	1H 3300	1

Clutch and gearbox

	Part No.	No. off
Competition clutch cover assembly	AEH 749	1
Competition clutch driven plate assembly	AEH 750	1
Graphite thrust bearing assembly	7H 3141	1
Graphite thrust bearing retaining spring	22B 66	1
Gearbox dipstick (with sealing rings)	AEC 3683	1

COMPETITION EQUIPMENT

Engine	Part No.	No. off
Crankshaft (induction-hardened heavy-duty material)	12H 1167	1
Camshaft (competition)	AEH 714	1
Main bearing (Extra clearance, lead-indium type) ..	AEH 808	6
	(set of 6 halves	
	8G 8843)	1
Packing piece—oil relief valve spring (·1 in. [2·54 mm.] thick)	AEH 798	1
Valve guide—inlet (Hidural)	AEH 755	4
Valve guide—exhaust (Hidural)	AEH 756	4
Inlet valve—1 $\frac{9}{16}$ in. (39·7 mm.) dia. (Nimonic) ..	AEH 757	4
Exhaust valve—1 $\frac{11}{32}$ in. (34·1 mm.) dia. (Nimonic) ..	AEH 758	4
Valve spring—outer (140 lb. [63·5 kg.]) ⎤ double	AHH 7264	8
Valve spring—inner (60 lb. [27·2 kg.]) ⎦ valve springs	AHH 7265	8
Valve spring top cup ⎤ for Nimonic valve ..	AEH 760	8
Valve spring bottom cup ⎦ and double springs ..	AEH 801	8
Valve collets—pairs (for Nimonic valve)	AEH 761	8
Valve springs, triple (set of 3)	AHH 7309	8
Valve spring top cup (for triple springs)	AHH 7313	8
Rocker shaft bracket—front	AEH 762	1
Rocker shaft bracket—rear	AEH 763	1
Distance piece for rocker—long	AEH 764	1
Distance piece for rockers—short	AEH 765	2
Tappet adjusting screw ($\frac{5}{16}$ in. UNF.)	AEH 766	8
Tappet	AEC 264	8
Push-rod	AEH 767	8
Cylinder head gasket (competition type)	AEH 768	1
Crankshaft chain wheel (steel)	AEH 769	1
Camshaft—high-lift—wide-period	AEH 770	1
Camshaft chain wheel (steel)	AEH 771	1
Flywheel complete (steel)	AEH 746	1
Connecting rod and cap complete—R.H. (cylinders 2 and 4)	AEH 642	2
Connecting rod bearing half	AEH 434	8
	(set of 8 halves	
	8G 2559	1
Connecting rod and cap complete—L.H. (cylinders 1 and 3)	AEH 644	2
Piston complete with gudgeon pin and rings	AEH 073603	4
Including:	(Grades 1 to 3)	
Piston ring—top	AEH 738	4
Piston ring—second and third	AEH 739	4
Piston ring—scraper	12H 759	4
Gudgeon pin	AEH 741	4
Circlip	AEH 742	8

COMPETITION EQUIPMENT

Engine ancillaries

	Part No.	No. off
Exhaust header (steel tube, tuned)	AHH 7103	1
Pulley (reduced speed) (for dynamo)	2A 864	1
Fan belt (for reduced speed pulley)	1G 2716	1
Distributor (competition tune) (distributor No. 40943A)	BHA 4415	1
Packing piece for pump strainer—1 in. (25·4 mm.) ..	AHH 7238	1
Engine oil sump (deep type) (to special order only) ..	AHH 7252	1

Parts for fitting Weber carburetter

	Part No.	No. off
Inlet manifold complete (for Weber carburetter) ..	AEH 772	1
Stud—carburetter to inlet manifold (long)	AEH 775	2
Stud—carburetter to inlet manifold (short)	AEH 776	2
Plain washer for stud	PWZ 105	4
Locknut for stud (thin type)	AEH 777	4
Stud—steady rod anchor plate to manifold	CLS 2511	4
Stud—throttle cable bracket to manifold	CHS 2511	2
Stud for petrol pump facing (anchor bracket) ..	FLS 2510	2
Stud for tachometer drive spindle housing	CLS 2511	1
Steady rod complete	AEH 778	2
Bolt—fork end to bracket or plate	HBZ 0510	4
Nut—fork end to bracket or plate	LNZ 205	4
Washer—fork end to bracket or plate	PWZ 105	4
Anchor plate—inlet manifold—front	AEH 782	1
Anchor plate—inlet manifold—rear	AEH 781	1
Nut—anchor plate—inlet manifold stud	LNZ 205	4
Washer—anchor plate	PWZ 105	4
Anchor bracket—steady rod front	AEH 783	1
Nut—anchor bracket stud	LNZ 205	2
Washer—anchor bracket stud	PWZ 105	2
Anchor bracket—steady rod rear	AEH 784	1
Carburetter assembly (Weber)	AEH 785	1
'O' ring—carburetter to manifold	AEA 605	2
Nut for carburetter stud	LNZ 205	4
Washer—carburetter stud	PWZ 105	4
Double-coil spring washer	AJD 7732	4
Adaptor union—petrol pipe to carburetter	AEH 786	1
Washer for adaptor	6K 638	1
Throttle countershaft—complete	AEH 787	1
Comprising:		
Throttle countershaft	AEH 788	1
Throttle lever—complete	AEH 789	1
Throttle lever	AEH 790	1
Ball pin (5/16 in. [7·9 mm.] dia.)	AUC 1153	1
Locating clip—throttle countershaft	AEH 791	1
Bracket—throttle cable abutment	AEH 792	1
Washer for stud—bracket to manifold	PWZ 105	2
Locknut for stud—bracket to manifold	LNZ 205	2
Adaptor—Servo brakes	AEH 793	1
Copper washer for adaptor	6K 638	1

COMPETITION EQUIPMENT

Parts for fitting Weber carburetter—*continued*				Part No.	No. off
Throttle link—lever to carburetter—complete			..	AEH 794	1
Comprising:					
Throttle link connecting rod ..	..	..	..	AEH 795	1
Ball joint socket (2 B.A.—R.H.)	..	..	..	AEC 2070	1
Ball joint socket (2 B.A.—L.H.)	..	..	..	AEH 796	1
Locknut (2 B.A.—R.H.)	..	..	..	AUC 2156	1
Locknut (2 B.A.—L.H.)	..	..	..	AEH 797	1

OPTIONAL EXTRAS

	Part No.
Overdrive	See Parts List
Wire wheels	See Parts List
Heater	See Parts List
Fresh-air unit	See Parts List
Fog lamp (Export only—Home through B.M.C. Service Ltd.)	57H 5593
Headlamp flasher..	See Parts List
Twin horns, low note (Export only—Home through B.M.C. Service Ltd.)	BCA 4726
Folding de-luxe hood	See Parts List
Oil cooler (standard for Export)	See Parts List
Tonneau cover	See Parts List
Anti-roll bar	See Parts List
Ashtray (Export only—Home through B.M.C. Service Ltd.)..	AHH 5539
Front bumper with over-riders (Export only—Home through B.M.C. Service Ltd.)	AHH 6917
Luggage grid ⌠(Export only—Home through B.M.C. Wing mirror ⌊ Service Ltd.)	AHH 6946
Wing mirror (Export only—Home through B.M.C. Service Ltd.)	27H 9863
Radio	See Trade List
Rear compartment cushion (Export only—Home through B.M.C. Service Ltd.)	See Parts List
Cigar-lighter (Export only—Home through B.M.C. Service Ltd.)	AHH 7010
Ace-Mercury wheel discs (Export only—Home through B.M.C. Service Ltd.) .. .. R.H.	AHH 7044
L.H.	AHH 7045
Long-range lamp (Export only—Home through B.M.C. Service Ltd.)	57H 5522
Steering-column locks (Germany, Sweden, Austria)	See Parts List
Hard Top ⌠Red	AHH 7152
Blue	AHH 7153
Grey	AHH 7220
White	AHH 7155
⌊Black	AHH 7154
Seat Harness	AHH 6208

ACCESSORIES

Foot-rest (passengers)

								Part No.
R.H.D.	Red	..	..	..	..	..	..	AHH 7112
	Blue	..	..	..	..	..	..	AHH 7113
	Black	..	..	..	..	..	..	AHH 7114
L.H.D.	Red	..	..	..	..	..	..	AHH 7116
	Blue	..	..	..	..	..	..	AHH 7117
	Black	..	..	..	..	..	..	AHH 7118
Map pocket	Red	..	..	..	..	..	..	AHH 7249
	Blue	..	..	..	..	..	..	AHH 7250
	Black	..	..	..	..	..	..	AHH 7251

Published by Brooklands Books Ltd., PO Box 146, Cobham,
Surrey KT11 1LG, England Phone: 01932 865051 Fax: 01932 868803
E-mail: sales@brooklands-books.com www.brooklands-books.com

Part Number: AKD 4034

ISBN 9780948207006   Ref: MG84HH   2298/9T4

OFFICIAL TECHNICAL BOOKS

Brooklands Technical Books has been formed to supply owners, restorers and professional repairers with official factory literature.

Workshop Manuals

Midget Instruction Manual		9781855200739
Midget TD & TF	AKD580A	9781870642552
MGA 1500 1600 & 1600 Mk. 2	AKD600D	9781869826307
MGA Twin Cam	AKD926B	9781855208179
Austin-Healey Sprite Mk. 2, Mk. 3 & Mk. 4 and		
MG Midget Mk. 1, Mk. 2 & Mk. 3		
	AKD4021	9781855202818
Midget 1500	AKM4071B	9781855201699
MGB & MGB GT	AKD3259 & AKD4957	9781855201743
MGB GT V8 Supplement		9781855201859
MGB, MGB GT and MGB GT V8		9781783180578
MGC	AKD 7133	9781855201828
Rover 25 & MG ZR 1999-2005		
	RCL0534ENGBB	9781855208834
Rover 75 & MG ZT 1999-2005		
	RCL0536ENGBB	9781855208841
MGF - 1.6 MPi, 1.8 MPi, 1.8VVC		
RCL 0051ENG, RCL0057ENG		
& RCL0124		9781855207165
MGF Electrical Manual 1996-2000 MY		
	RCL0341	9781855209077
MG TF	RCL0493	9781855207493

Parts Catalogues

MGA 1500	AKD1055	9781870642569
MGA 1600 Mk. 1 & Mk. 2	AKD1215	9781870642613
Austin-Healey Sprite Mk. 1 & Mk. 2 and		
MG Midget Mk. 1 (Mechanical & Body Edition)		
	AKD3566 & AKD3567	9781783180509
Austin-Healey Sprite Mk. 3 & Mk. 4 and		
MG Midget Mk. 2 & Mk. 3 (Mechanical & Body		
Edition 1969)	AKD3513 & AKD3514	9781783180554
Austin-Healey Sprite Mk. 3 & Mk. 4 and		
MG Midget Mk. 2 & Mk. 3 (Feb 1977 Edition)		
	AKM0036	9780948207419
MGB up to Sept 1976	AKM0039	9780948207068
MGB Sept 1976 on	AKM0037	9780948207440

Owners Handbooks

Midget Series TD		9781870642910
Midget TF and TF 1500		
Operation Manual	AKD658A	9781870642934
MGA 1500	AKD598G	9781855202924
MGA 1600	AKD1172C	9781855201668
MGA 1600 Mk. 2	AKD1958A	9781855201675
MGA Twin Cam (Operation)	AKD879	9781855207929
MGA Twin Cam (Operation)	AKD879B	9781855207936
MGA 1500 Special Tuning	AKD819A	9781783181728
MGA 1500 and 1600 Mk. 1 Special Tuning		
	AKD819B	9781783181735
Midget TF and TF 1500	AKD210A	9781855202979
Midget Mk. 3 (GB 1967-74)	AKD7596	9781855201477
Midget (Pub 1978)	AKM3229	9781855200906
Midget Mk. 3 (US 1967-74)	AKD7883	9781855206311
Midget Mk. 3 (US 1976)	AKM3436	9781855201767
Midget Mk. 3 (US 1979)	AKM4386	9781855201774
MGB Tourer (Pub 1965)	AKD3900C	9781869826741

MGB Tourer & GT (Pub 1969)	AKD3900J	9781855200609
MGB Tourer & GT (Pub 1974)	AKD7598	9781869826727
MGB Tourer & GT (Pub 1976)	AKM3661	9781869826703
MGB GT V8	AKD8423	9781869826710
MGB Tourer & GT (US 1968)	AKD7059B	9781870642514
MGB Tourer & GT (US 1971)	AKD7881	9781870642521
MGB Tourer & GT (US 1973)	AKD8155	9781870642538
MGB Tourer (US 1975)	AKD3286	9781870642545
MGB (US 1979)	AKM8098	9781855200722
MGB Tourer & GT Tuning	CAKD4034L	9780948207051
MGB Special Tuning 1800cc	AKD4034	9780948207006
MGC	AKD4887B	9781869826734
MGF (Modern shape)	RCL0332ENG	9781855208339

Owners Workshop Manuals - Autobooks

MGA & MGB & GT 1955-1968	
(Glove Box Autobooks Manual)	9781855200937
MGA & MGB & GT 1955-1968	
(Autobooks Manual)	9781783180356
Austin-Healey Sprite Mk. 1, 2, 3 & 4 and	
MG Midget Mk. 1, 2, 3 & 1500 1958-1980	
(Glove Box Autobooks Manual)	9781855201255
Austin-Healey Sprite Mk. 1, 2, 3 & 4 and	
MG Midget Mk. 1, 2, 3 & 1500 1958-1980	
(Autobooks Manual)	9781783180332
MGB & MGB GT 1968-1981	
(Glove Box Autobooks Manual)	9781855200944
MGB & MGB GT 1968-1981	
(Autobooks Manual)	9781783180325

Carburetters

SU Carburetters Tuning Tips & Techniques	
	9781855202559
Solex Carburetters Tuning Tips & Techniques	
	9781855209770
Weber Carburettors Tuning Tips and Techniques	
	9781855207592

Restoration Guide

MG T Series Restoration Guide	9781855202115
MGA Restoration Guide	9781855203020
Restoring Sprites & Midgets	9781855205987
Practical Classics On MGB Restoration	9780946489428

MG - Road Test Books

MG Gold Portfolio 1929-1939	9781855201941
MG TA & TC GOLD PORT 1936-1949	9781855203150
MG TD & TF Gold Portfolio 1949-1955	9781855203167
MG Y-Type & Magnette Road Test Portfolio	9781855208629
MGB & MGC GT V8 GP 1962-1980	9781855200715
MGA & Twin Cam Gold Portfolio 1955-1962	9781855200784
MGB Roadsters 1962-1980	9781869826109
MGC & MGB GT V8 LEX	9781855203631
MG Midget Road Test Portfolio 1961-1979	9781855208957
MGF & TF Performance Portfolio 1995-2005	9781855207073
Road & Track On MG Cars 1949-1961	9780946489398
Road & Track On MG Cars 1962-1980	9780946489817

From MG specialists, Amazon and all good motoring bookshops.

Brooklands Books Ltd., P.O. Box 146, Cobham, Surrey, KT11 1LG, England, UK

www.brooklandsbooks.com

Printed and bound in Great Britain by
Marston Book Services Ltd, Oxfordshire

Printed by Printforce, United Kingdom